Tom is brave

Story by Beverley Randell

Illustrated by Ernest Papps

Tom went to the store for Mom.

Tom! Tom!

Look where you are going!

Look where you are going!

"Oh! Oh! **Oh!**"

Tom cried and cried.

Tom went home.

"Look, Mom!

I am **bleeding**!"

"Oh, Tom!" said Mom.

"Here you are," said Mom. "You **are** brave."

Tom went into the store.
"Look!" he said.

"Look at me!"